WHAT'S INSIDE

INTRODUCTION
Why Media Is Important

Running a national service program is more than a full-time job. Between developing projects, recruiting volunteers, managing finances, seeking resources, and filling out paperwork, it may feel like there's no time to do anything else. With all the things a busy program manager has to do, you may wonder: "Why should I care about media coverage, and can it really help me?"

The answer is yes – and getting it is easier than you think. Every year, thousands of stories about Senior Corps, AmeriCorps, and Learn and Serve America appear in the media – almost all generated by local project staff and volunteers. You don't have to be a media pro to get good coverage, but having some tips and resources can help. That's the purpose of this guide.

Publicizing your program in not a goal in itself. It's a means of building support for your program and increasing your likelihood of success. Taking the time to communicate with the public helps attract resources from your community, including volunteers, sponsors, and funding, and helps educate people about your program.

All of us engage in public relations each time we tell people about what we do. You probably already have a good idea how to tailor messages about your program and achievements to a specific audience. If you are talking to a potential volunteer, you might convey the personal satisfaction gained from giving back to your community. If you're talking to a potential recipient of your services, you would point out the benefits you provide to individuals and organizations. These scenarios are good examples of effective public relations. Public relations simply means developing and managing a deliberate and strategic approach to publicizing your message. Ultimately, a good public relations campaign will create a mutually beneficial relationship between your program and your audiences. Maintaining relationships with media outlets will help you be a voice for those you serve, and strengthen your organization as a trusted and credible resource in your community.

We are living in an information age. Therefore, targeting the news media has become one of the most effective methods for transmitting information to the public. You already know the types of media out there: television, radio, newspapers, the Internet, newsletters, and specialty magazines. What you may not know is that not all types of media are right for disseminating all types of information to all types of people. This is especially true given the thousands of other organizations competing alongside you for the public's attention. That's why it's necessary to apply a strategic approach to your public relations to determine:

1. Who your audience is and what their opinions, attitudes, and perceptions are

2. Which types of media can best reach your audience

3. What is the best way to shape your message for each type of media

Your job doesn't stop with the answers to these questions. Reaching the media takes strategic planning as well. Helping you develop a good public relations plan and execute that plan is what this guidebook is all about. This guidebook includes answers to many frequently asked questions, and offers tips and ideas for people new to public relations and those interested in learning new ideas for broadcasting their message.

The main section of this guidebook contains:

> Brief descriptions of the various types of media outlets

> Pointers on conducting media outreach, including developing a media plan, selling your story to reporters (often referred to as "pitching"), putting together a good press list, and getting your event on your local calendar listings of events that reporters use to decide what to cover.

> Tips on building and maintaining relationships with reporters

> Useful pointers for interviews

> Advice on communicating through public service announcements (PSAs)

We've also provided a number of appendices for easy reference, including:

> Tips on writing news releases and hosting news conferences

> A variety of sample media materials

> Lists of important print media outlets

> A sample media list and media sign-in sheet

We hope this guidebook will take some of the mystery out of working with the media. We also we hope you realize the value that positive media coverage can bring to your program. By taking your message to a wider audience, you can leverage new partners, recruit more volunteers, gain more public support, and increase your program's long-term sustainability and success. And every time your local project gets positive coverage, you help advance the national service movement as a whole. National service is still largely unknown, and we need you to help tell the story.

No media guidebook will answer every question. So when you get stuck or have a media question that's not addressed here, give the Office of Public Affairs at the Corporation for National and Community Service a call at 202-606-5000. Also, be sure to visit the newsroom at *www.nationalservice.gov* for the latest news, information, and resources to help you tell your national service story. We're here to help! ■

TYPES OF MEDIATYPES OF MEDIA

Today, there are many more types of media than there were 10 years ago. Most people still get their news from traditional forms of media such as television, newspapers, magazines and radio. A growing number of people get their news and information from the Internet. Understanding each type of media and its target audience is a crucial first step to putting your public relations plan in motion. You should also have an idea of which media your target audiences are most likely to use. We have provided an overview of each type of media below.

NEWSPAPERS

Newspapers provide ongoing, up-to-date coverage of national and local stories. Placing your story in a newspaper is a great way to reach potential volunteers, as well as decision makers in your community, such as business leaders, elected officials and experts. Newspaper editors and reporters are usually looking for story ideas where you can provide information on the "who," "what," "when," "where," "why" and "how" of the story. Specifically:

> **Who** is the story about and whom does it affect?

> **What** is happening and why is it newsworthy?

> **When** is the story occurring? Did it happen already or will it happen in the future?

> **Where** is the story taking place? Is it national or local?

> **Why** does this story matter? Why should readers care?

> **How** does this story affect the community? How does it affect the nation?

There are typically two types of newspapers in your community—daily and weekly. Daily newspapers are divided into distinct sections, including national news, local news, features, editorials, columns, opinion editorials (also known as op-eds), and letters to the editor. Op-eds or letters to the editor can be written by you or one of your supporters to express an opinion on issues of particular importance to your organization. Weeklies may have the same format, but items will be reported over a longer period of time. Before you pitch a story to a newspaper, know how often it is published and who it reaches. This will help determine your angle, or "news hook," and which publication will most likely be interested in what you have to offer.

Daily newspapers often target larger metropolitan areas and focus on a wide variety of news. Some of the major dailies will even have editions that are tailored to submarkets or regions within the larger metropolitan area. These papers have much larger staffs than weekly publications and often seek information from a variety of sources. Daily newspapers will rarely publish submitted information exactly as submitted. You should make a point to know as much as you can about the reporters you are pitching—what their "beat" is and how they might cover your story.

Weekly papers are more commonly located in smaller communities and concentrate more on local news. Weeklies have much smaller staffs than their daily counterparts and, as a result, are often more open to publishing materials as submitted.

MAGAZINES

Magazines, like newspapers, focus on stories with detailed and fact-driven information and often report on a particular angle of the story that will be most interesting to their audience. This means that when you pitch a story to a magazine, you must be sure to tailor it to each magazine's target audience. Special interest or community magazines in your area will be especially receptive to what your program has to offer and what you are doing in the community. Make sure to become familiar with the magazines published in your city or region and identify those that would be most receptive to your program and activities.

Unlike newspapers, magazines require a much longer lead time for their stories. Often, a story will hit the newsstands several months after it is pitched. This requires you to plan far in advance for the types of stories that are well-suited for magazines, such as personal profiles of volunteers or significant results from a new initiative.

WIRE SERVICES

Wire services are the nerve center of the media. They typically compile stories from many different sources and post them for their member journalists' use. You probably have heard of the Associated Press (AP). AP has both print and broadcast (television and radio) divisions that feed stories and content to their members. Most media outlets in the United States are members of one of the major news services (AP, Reuters and United Press International). AP has a bureau in each state and should be contacted when you have news that's appropriate for a statewide audience. AP and other general news wire services rely on information sent to them by organizations just like yours. There are also specific wire services that are solely dedicated to posting stories on particular topics, like health, technology, and the nonprofit sector.

An up-to-date listing of state-by-state AP bureaus can be found at:
www.ap.org/pages/contact/contact.html

TELEVISION

Television is regarded as the media vehicle with the furthest reach, but with a growing number of cable stations, it is important to choose a television outlet or program based on its audience and then tailor your message to fit its scope of coverage.

National network news stations (i.e., ABC, CBS, NBC) often focus on national stories only, featuring in-depth stories that are either high profile or investigative. This is generally the same for cable news stations, such as CNN, FOX News, and MSNBC.

On the other hand, the local affiliates of both national and cable news stations spend a large chunk of airtime focusing on local issues. It is a good idea to contact them about a local event or initiative you are organizing.

Successful television pitches, more so than print pitches, require a visual element to the story. Hosting an event, hanging a banner, or inviting reporters to witness a volunteer activity are all good ways to provide a visual for television cameras.

If your story idea or event reaches beyond your local community, and you believe it could be of interest to people in other cities and/or states, a B-roll distribution or satellite media tour (SMT) can help spread your message throughout a specific region or the entire country.

B-roll is a compilation of video footage of your program in action. The footage can include a special event, a news conference, or a taped series of sound bites featuring your program's spokesperson speaking about a particular issue or topic. Stations use the footage to complement their stories. You can create your own B-roll package by shooting footage at specific events, or you can invite news stations to film their own footage at a news event or program activity.

An SMT is a series of television interviews with your program's spokesperson conducted via satellite by stations across the country. They are often produced by a production company. Within a short period of time (usually two to three hours), your spokesperson can deliver your program's message directly to target audiences all over the country.

RADIO

Like all forms of media, there are more radio stations today than ever before, and most tailor their programming to a specific audience. Determining your area stations' format and audience is an important step to including radio outreach in your public relations strategy. Those stations that include talk radio and news segments are the prime radio stations you should target to cover in depth aspects of your program or to interview one of your spokespeople on the air. If you are pitching a public service announcement, you can (and in most cases should) expand your radio outreach to stations that only have music programming. To learn more about public service announcements and when to use them, see "Communication through Public Service Announcements" on page 20.

A good way to reach a large number of radio stations is through a radio media tour (RMT) or audio news release (ANR). An RMT is similar to an SMT in that radio stations interview your spokesperson remotely during a scheduled period of time. To reach an even wider number of radio stations, you can create an ANR, which can be distributed across the country, potentially reaching millions of people.

PUBLIC AFFAIRS PROGRAMS

Both radio and TV stations have public affairs shows that are designed to take an in-depth look at community news and often involve interviews, panel discussions, and commentaries. These types of programs can be a great way to get publicity. Local public affairs programs are often on cable access stations or a part of your public radio station's lineup. You can tie in a pitch with a day of service, an annual event such as back to school, or a holiday. For example, if you have a program serving veterans, you could pitch public affairs shows that will air around Veterans Day or Memorial Day. The shows are likely to do something on those topics, so take advantage of it.

While it never hurts to send materials for upcoming events to appropriate local public affairs shows, they—like their national counterparts—usually plan their schedules well in advance. You will be most successful with public affairs shows when you position your organization as a resource for future programming. For more information on how to establish yourself and your organization as a resource to reporters, check out "Reporters: Building and Maintaining Relationships" on page 15.

INTERNET/WEBSITES

In today's fast-paced world, the Internet—specifically news-oriented websites—are becoming a heavily relied upon source for easily accessed, reliable, and up-to-date information. Like most of the media vehicles we have discussed, websites are targeted toward a specific audience, so be sure to take the time to understand where your target audience is gathering information online before you begin your pitch.

Reporters often use an organization's website to find out information and identify potential story ideas. For this reason, you should maintain an up-to-date website with information both reporters and the general community will find useful. A catchy design for your site is important. Web-savvy volunteers may want to try their hand at designing a website for you. Be sure to keep your contact information updated so that reporters are able to reach you easily.

It is a good idea to make your communications available on your website in a designated "online press room." The press room should include press releases, background information, fact sheets, event listings, links to other useful community websites and contact information. The site could also include profiles of volunteers who share their story about assisting people in your community. The profiles help your organization come to life and inspire others to volunteer. Always remember to keep contact information and FAQs up to date and easy to find.

Most major national and local television, print, and radio outlets have an online presence. While many news websites carry the same name as a major print or television outlet, this does not mean that the same editors and reporters work for both. For example, you could successfully get a story placed on CNN.com that never makes it to CNN, the cable television station. In addition, some print outlets will report a story on their website, but will choose not to publish it in the print edition. If you intend to secure a story with the traditional news outlet as well as the online version, you will more often than not need to pitch both types of outlets.

When tracking online media coverage, you should check the websites on the same day of your event or planned media outreach. Websites are constantly updated and have different rules on access to archived stories. It is best to copy the articles into a document to save them and insure that you have accurate documentation of all media coverage.

NEWSLETTERS

Newsletters are an excellent way to reach a very targeted audience. Your program newsletter can help introduce new volunteers and other organization supporters to your program. Use your newsletter to share the stories of volunteers, report on special events, and keep your community apprised of recent

■ TYPES OF MEDIA

happenings within your program. Invite local chapters of organizations with a similar or related mission to submit stories to your newsletter.

Another option is to submit stories about your program to other organizational newsletters. For example, many churches and synagogues distribute weekly bulletins or monthly newsletters featuring community calendars. You could work with them to include your program events in these calendars. This will help establish relationships with other organizations and allow you to share information about your program with a broader audience. ■

MEDIA OUTREACH

So, your program is incredible and you have amazing volunteers, dedicated community partners, and a list of accomplishments a mile high. What next? Spreading the word about your program and your accomplishments lets people know about the great things your program is doing.

Whether your goal is to raise awareness of your program, promote a specific event, highlight accomplishments, or recruit new volunteers or members, a media plan can help your program reach thousands of people—including potential volunteers, prospective funders, local and state officials, and potential partners. An effective plan can generate print, broadcast, and electronic coverage of your program, and help cultivate relationships with local television, radio, and print reporters, leading to ongoing interest in your program.

Developing a Media Plan

An effective media plan will address three basic questions:

What are your public relations goals?

The first step in developing a media plan is to determine your long-term goals. These goals will help you determine your messages, as well as what media you'll want to target. When determining your goals, keep the following questions in mind:

> What are you trying to do? Recruit new members? Increase program awareness?
> Build public support for your program?

> Who are your audiences?

> What are the main messages you want to communicate?

> If you could write the headlines, what would they be?

> What resources—staff, contacts, materials—are needed to communicate with the media?

A number of resources, including customizable templates, are included in this guidebook. However, the availability of resources like program staff and staff time is another important factor to consider when developing your plan. Determining the resources you have available for media efforts will help you build on existing tools and opportunities, and set realistic goals.

> What materials and tools do you already have?

> What media contacts and relationships do you already have?

> Which staff members are available and how much can time can they devote
> to media-related activities?

> What is your estimated budget for media relations?

> Can your partner organizations provide assistance, resources or spokespeople?

> Do you have a list of volunteers, members, and alumni who would be willing to speak to the media?

> Are there other community leaders or organizations that can speak on behalf of your program?

What is your timeline?

Consider your program's calendar of events, the National Service calendar, and your local community calendar to determine what events and activities will provide the best media opportunities for your program throughout the year. Be sure to include activities that all national service programs take part in, such as Make a Difference Day, Martin Luther King Day and National Volunteer Week. Also consider the following questions to determine other newsworthy opportunities:

> What activities and events are already planned to take place throughout the year?

> Do certain activities traditionally attract more attention than others?

> What activities or events best showcase your program's strengths and contributions to the community?

> What activities are your volunteers or members most excited about?

> Which activities involve collaboration with other organizations, businesses, or community members?

> Will studies or results be released that you would like to promote?

> What opportunities exist to collaborate with other programs?

NEXT STEPS

Once you have determined your goals, opportunities and resources, you can set a strategy and adhere to a timeline. An outreach strategy will help you determine what, how, and when to communicate with the media. Keeping your overall media plan in mind, your strategy should:

> Identify who will be interested in the story

> Identify which media outlets reach these audiences

> Determine how to pitch or package the story as a newsworthy event

> Identify key messages and spokespeople

> Develop written materials to promote your program or event

> Set a timeline for outreach

> Determine a plan for tracking and follow-up

The following sections will guide you through these steps by offering ideas on how to get information to the media, identify and work with the right reporters, make the most of an interview, and communicate through public service announcements. Refer to the "Appendices" section for template press materials and timelines to guide your outreach efforts.

Tips

> **Keep a list of "validators" who can speak enthusiastically about your program.** Volunteers, community leaders, and others who have seen the benefits your program provides first hand are among your most valuable resources. Keep a running list of these and other individuals who you can point reporters to and who can act as validators for your program. Depending on your community, consider having a validator who is fluent in a second language, especially if you are targeting ethnic media.

> **Reporters love numbers and data.** When it comes down to it, a reporter's job is to present the facts. When thinking about your plan, include a method for collecting any data a reporter may find interesting. For example: How many seniors did your program assist in the last activity/month/year? How many meals/houses/projects did your volunteers serve/build/complete? Has there been an evaluation showing improvements in children's test scores, attendance or participation in activities?

> **Designate a communications team.** Communicating with the media is a team effort. Designate and train a communications team with clear roles and responsibilities and clear guidelines on how to pitch the story. Remember, your media outreach team could be quoted by a reporter, so be sure that each member of your team is well versed in the same messages and talking points.

How do you prepare a pitch?

> **Compile a press list.** Your list should contain the appropriate newsroom personnel or beat reporters/producers to contact. (See "Tips on Developing Press Lists and Newsroom Contacts" below.)

> **Develop a set of pitch points.** These are the main ideas that you will focus on to sell your story.

When do you pitch the media?

> **One to two months before an event or activity:** Call your local newspapers and television programs to determine their lead times for specific sections or programs. For example, many newspapers have longer lead times for their religion, business and entertainment/events sections. Local television programs also develop a list of potential program topics several weeks in advance.

> **One week before an event or activity:** Fax or e-mail the news advisory to everyone on your list. Make follow-up calls to pitch the event and gauge media interest.

> **The day before the event:** Send the advisory again and call contacts that you have not spoken with yet.

> **The morning of the event or activity:** Call again just to find out who is attending. Fax or email your news release at the conclusion of your event.

TIPS ON DEVELOPING PRESS LISTS AND NEWSROOM CONTACTS

How Do You Build a Media List?

There are a variety of media outlets in your community that you can include in your press list. If you do not have access to an existing list, it is easy to create one. You can begin by looking in your local phone book for listings of TV and radio stations and local daily and weekly newspapers and magazines. You can also use the U.S. Newspaper List website at *www.usnpl.com*, or search for media outlets on web portals such as Yahoo or Google. Media directories such as Bacon's Media Guide and the News Media Yellow Book can be found at your local library. In addition, you can subscribe to online services that offer current information on media outlets throughout the country. These are useful, and cost-effective, if you send information to many media outlets on a frequest basis.

Print

In addition to the local newspaper, remember to include smaller media outlets on your list, including community newspapers, weekly newspapers, and university newspapers. Newsletters that cover your area of service or reach your audience might be another resource to consider. If your project serves local youth, consider pitching to the school district's newsletter. If you have a bureau of the Associated Press wire service in your community, add the bureau chiefs or assignment editors to the list. To check if you have a bureau office in your community, visit www.ap.org/pages/contact/contact.html. In addition, some communities have local business journals that cover community-specific news.

Television

Include on your media list all of the television stations in your community that offer local news or community-based programming, as well as the public broadcasting stations. In addition to news programming, see if the stations air minority, business, religious, or other public affairs programming.

Determine who the local cable providers are. Find out whether they have their own public affairs station in their channel lineup and determine who the appropriate contacts are. Finally, some communities have their own local cable news networks; check to see if yours does.

Radio

Find out which local radio stations air news reports or have news or public affairs programming. In addition to news programming, find out whether the stations air minority, business, religious or other public affairs programming. As you develop your list, make sure you note the type of radio station it is (i.e., news, public affairs, talk, music with some news). This will help you when you make your pitch. In addition, find out whether there is a state radio network in your state and determine who the news director is for the network.

Once you have the list of media outlets you want to include in your press list, call each outlet to determine the appropriate media contact. At the very least, locate the names of the reporters and producers who cover community news (your first priority). Depending on the focus of your program, other beats may also be important, including religion, education, family issues, philanthrophy, and the environment. If your target audience includes members of minority communities, remember to identify reporters and media outlets that cover those communities as well. In addition, identify the editors of the op-ed and editorial pages of the local newspaper, as well as the local columnists and feature writers who might take an interest in some aspect of your program's focus.

Compile the name, beat or title, phone number, fax number, and e-mail address for each person. You can also include information about the best method and time for contacting them. If you are planning a specific event in the community, other people to contact include:

> **Print:** City editor, editorial page editor, columnists who have an interest in community issues, writers for the calendar or community events page, and photo editor (for particularly visual events or events where prominent local citizens will be participating.)
> **TV:** Planning editors, assignment editors, reporters/on-air personalities, producers of specific shows including morning shows, community programs, or minority-themed news and public affairs programs.
> **Radio:** News directors, assignment desk staff, public affairs show hosts and producers, and on-air personalities.

DON'T FORGET THE DAYBOOK

What Is the Daybook?

The daybook provides members of the media with a daily calendar of media events happening in and around a city or state. News services, like the Associated Press, maintain a daybook and distribute it through their wire services to journalists nationwide. In addition to a national daybook, AP publishes state and local versions. Newsroom managers, assignment editors and reporters from other media outlets check the daybook many times each day for the latest updates on important events happening throughout the region.

A daybook listing looks similar to this:

September 12, 2004
Community Service
Corporation for National and Community Service
Discussion, "The Next Ten Years: What the Future Holds for National Service"
Participants: David Eisner, CEO, Corporation for National and Community Service; members of the National Service Community
Location: Corporation for National and Community Service, 1201 New York Ave., 10th Floor, Washington, DC, 10 a.m. (September 12, 2004)
Contact: The Office of Public Affairs, 202-606-5000

How can you make certain that your media events get listed on the daybook?

You must pitch your activity to the daybook editor in advance of the event in order to have it placed on the calendar of news events for a specific day. Getting the event on the daybook tells journalists in your community that an event is happening, lets them know who will be participating, and gives them a hint about the news that will be released. Pitching a daybook editor should not replace contacting other AP reporters or local print and broadcast media outlets about your event.

How to pitch and place stories on the Associated Press daybook

1. Pitch events that include one or all of the following elements:

   > New and newsworthy information, such as the release of new data, the announcement of strong community involvement in one of your initiatives, or a news conference with local dignitaries

   > Media-friendly activities that are visually appealing (e.g., a health fair, youth build or clean-up effort)

   > A schedule of your activities, including a list of spokespeople who are available to speak to reporters about your event or story idea

2. Prepare a news advisory with the "who," "what," "when" and "where" of your event as well as any other information to be included in the daybook listing. (See Appendix G for a sample media advisory.)

3. Consult the state-by-state listing of AP bureaus at www.ap.org/pages/contact/contact.html.

4. Call the daybook editor, pitch your event, and fax or e-mail a copy of your news advisory to the bureau at least one week in advance of the event. While daybooks are updated on a regular basis, most reporters look at the Monday daybook to plan their week. Make sure the advisory is sent to the daybook by the Friday prior to the event.

5. Follow up with the daybook editor by phone or e-mail to find out if your event is listed. When you are contacting the daybook editor, you might say, "I'm just checking if my event is on the daybook."

6. When you are contacting local reporters, refer to the daybook listing in your pitch. For example, you might say "You may have seen our event on the AP daybook. I'm calling to give you additional information about ..."

7. Update the daybook editor if there are changes in your event location or time or if prominent speakers join your efforts. ■

REPORTERS
Building and Maintaining Relationships

Building and maintaining relationships with reporters is essential to getting your messages out in the media. Having strong relationships with reporters helps position your organization front and center in your community. It helps you gain coverage of your organization's activities and gets your message into stories that relate to the valuable work you are doing. If you want to draw a reporter's attention to neglected needs in the community and how you're helping to meet those needs, a well-developed rapport will enable you to do that. It will also increase the likelihood that the reporter will contact you for comments. Using the following tips will help you build these relationships that are so key to your outreach efforts.

BUILDING THE RELATIONSHIP

Do Your Homework

After you've identified the right reporters in your community to develop relationships with, read their stories and learn as much as you can about the news outlet where they work. Does the reporter have a specific beat or do they focus on several different issue areas? How big is the media outlet where they work? Do the reporter's stories get picked up by other publications (possibly as a result of a media partnership)?

Send a Press Packet

Providing the right reporter with information on your program should be your first step in introducing your program to the newsroom. This keeps you from having to cold call reporters and also allows them to have your contact information handy. You want to demonstrate the resources your organization can provide, so your packet should include the following:

> One-page backgrounder on your organization

> One-page Corporation program fact sheet that relates to your organization
(i.e., AmeriCorps*VISTA, Senior Corps, etc.)

> Previously published news clippings that mention your organization (be sure they are positive)

> Your contact information

Give Them a Call

After you have sent a press packet, give each reporter a call. Rather than simply asking whether they received your press packet, use this opportunity to introduce yourself and your organization and how you can be a resource to them. Let them know that they can contact you if they have any questions about topics that relate to your program or about national service in general. You can also share with them any upcoming events that you might be having. However, keep the focus primarily on you and your organization as a resource in this relationship-building phase.

Meet with the Reporter

For those reporters with whom you would like to form a closer relationship, finding the opportunity to meet is the next step in building a relationship. Consider inviting the reporter to lunch or coffee. If you live in a smaller media market, you may want to set up meetings with all the community beat reporters at your local paper. Reporters may also be interested in seeing your program and your volunteers or members in action. You could schedule a site visit of your program facility or project. If you are building or renovating something, give reporters a chance to see and experience it. If you have a large number of reporters on your list, you should identify the most important contacts and focus on them.

What to say and bring to a reporter meeting:

Allow the reporter to ask questions. This is their time to explore the issues and pose the questions they've never had a chance to ask.

Bring a press packet with information on your program, the appropriate one-page Corporation program fact sheet, news clippings, and your contact information.

Don't control the conversation. This is your time to build a relationship with the reporter, so your conversation should be a back and forth on what each of you do, activities in the community, and how you can be a resource to each other.

MAINTAINING THE RELATIONSHIP

Be a Resource to Reporters

In order to establish yourself and your program as a credible resource to reporters, you will need to provide them with the information they need by their deadline. When they call, take the request, ask what their deadline is, and get the needed information back to them within that time frame. This will improve the chances that they will keep your name and number in their Rolodex.

Keep a Current Media Log

In order to keep track of a reporter's contact information, media outlet, requests, and deadlines, it's a good idea to keep a log that you can refer to and that can be shared with colleagues to keep everyone on the same page. While a sign-in sheet (see Appendix K) is used to track reporter attendance at an event, a log contains more in-depth information. It includes special notes related to the reporters' individual deadlines, preferences, and any stories the reporter has written on your program.

Provide Reporters with Up-to-Date, Newsworthy Information

Make a point of keeping reporters in the loop on what's going on with your local program and upcoming events. Be sure that you keep your updates to what is timely and newsworthy so your calls to reporters don't become a general update. Provide just enough information to keep them hooked and interested in what you have to offer.

BASIC TIPS ON WORKING WITH REPORTERS

Below are a few pointers on working with reporters, including the best time to pitch, and what to do before, during, and after an interview.

When to Contact the Media

Print

It is best to call a newsroom between 10:00 a.m. and 2:00 p.m., when reporters are likely to be available and not on deadline.

Television

Planning editors generally take calls between 10:00 a.m. and 3:00 p.m., but not around noontime when they are putting together their mid-day news show. It is best to call the assignment desk after the morning planning meeting, which usually ends between 9:30 and 10:00 a.m. Don't forget to describe the story's visuals when making your pitch.

Radio

The best time to call is early in the morning—between 7:30 and 8:30 a.m. After that, the staff goes into planning meetings. You can make another round of calls at about 10:00 a.m. News directors, reporters and producers are often gone by the afternoon. If you are pitching a specific press conference or event and the reporter is not able to attend, offer to have one of your spokespeople do a taped interview.

Online media

Reporters who write for online publications often have revolving deadlines, but, as a general rule, you should follow the same rules that apply to print reporters. Call between 10:00 a.m. and 2:00 p.m.

Preparing for an Interview

> **Develop three to five messages or talking points.** These are the main ideas you want to emphasize and repeat during your interview. Weave these points into all of your answers. Anticipate what questions may be asked and be prepared with the answers. If you are successful at "staying on message," you will be better able to determine the shape of the news coverage.

> **Learn more about the interview.** Ask what the reporter is looking for. What is the goal of the story? Will this be live or on tape? If it's a radio interview, will listeners be calling in to ask questions? Or, if it's a TV talk show interview, will there be other guests or panelists? Who are they? What are their backgrounds?

> **Understand the reporter's timeline.** Find out when the reporter must complete the story and plan your interview accordingly. You should plan to accommodate the reporter's deadline, so they won't feel rushed and your interview will go more smoothly. A lot of print reporting is done by phone. If a reporter calls you at an inconvenient time, you can ask to reschedule for a more appropriate time. Also, prior to the interview, find out if the reporter is talking to anyone else about the story.

> **Choose a location.** You may want to ask the reporter to conduct the interview at your program office or project site, so they can observe your working environment. Print reporters are most likely to visit you on site, though television and radio reporters may want to do the interview on site to film footage or capture sound. In this case, you should carefully review which parts of your program site should be made available to the reporter. For some interviews, most often those for television and radio, you will be required to visit a studio. In this case, you should arrive early to prepare for the interview.

> **Wear the right clothing.** Since the reporters are interested in learning about your program and the people involved with it, you should dress as you would at your program office or project site to give them insight into your typical environment. For example, AmeriCorps members can wear their uniforms for interviews. All dress, however, should be conservative and neat.

> **Relax and focus.** Breathing exercises may feel silly, but they will go a long way toward helping you feel calm. Get to your location 10-15 minutes early and spend time practicing your core message points.

General interview tips

> Be enthusiastic

> Avoid jargon or technical language

> Maintain eye contact with the reporter

> Keep your answers succinct

> Nothing you say is "off the record"

> Never say "no comment"

> Don't repeat negative words or inaccurate facts included in a reporter's question

> Don't worry about repeated questions

> If you don't know the answer to a question, say so

> If the answer is "no," it's ok to say "no"

Special Tips for Broadcast Interviews

Use a conversational tone. Avoid reading from your notes. This technique will help keep you relaxed and build rapport between you and the reporter.

Use your voice. Remember to change your tone to emphasize your message points. By using inflection, you can make the key ideas stand out.

Keep your answers brief. The average broadcast sound bite is 10-15 seconds. Stick to your three to five message points and then stop talking.

For taped stories, ask to do it again if you didn't like your answer. If the interview isn't live and you've fumbled an answer, tell the reporter you think you can do it better if they ask the question again. Reporters want the sharpest sound bite for their story, so they will often give you the chance to answer again.

Ask for water. If your mouth or throat gets dry, you will be glad it is there during the interview. But be careful. Drinking too much too quickly not only looks sloppy, it could send a message that you are uncomfortable.

Television Interviews

Wear the right clothes. Women should avoid wearing elaborate jewelry, neon-bright colors or clothing with repeating patterns. Men should not wear white or striped shirts.

Be aware of your posture. If you are sitting at a desk, keep your arms on the tabletop and do not tap your hands. If you are standing face-to-face with the reporter, keep your feet about shoulder-width apart and your hands at your side. If you are seated, don't swivel in the chair or sway. The most important rule: be natural.

Never look at the camera. Keep eye contact with the reporter. Looking away or averting your eyes connotes that you are uncomfortable or untrustworthy. There is no need to talk down to the microphone—it will pick up your voice.

Be careful about nodding your head. Besides the fact that it looks jarring, it implies that you agree with what a reporter may be saying. Also, refrain from waving your arms during an interview. The camera angle is probably not wide enough to capture your movements.

Remain upbeat. Your compassion and commitment to your program is your best asset. Smile when appropriate. Stay focused and positive.

Consider wearing make-up or powder on your face. The bright lights of television will make you look paler than you are normally. If you are offered powder, take advantage of it. Avoid looking shiny on television.

Never frown. Television cameras tend to exaggerate facial expressions. A neutral facial expression can often appear like an angry or sad one.

Remember: The Corporation's Office of Public Affairs can help you with tips on potentially tough reporter questions. If in doubt, give us a call at 202-606-5000.

After the Interview

A small but important way to help build a relationship with a reporter is to send a short thank you note to the reporter who interviewed you and others who may have been involved, like a producer or the media outlet's general manager. Express your gratitude for the interview and offer yourself as a resource to them in the future. If you have ideas for other stories, you could also include them in the note. And don't forget to record your interview experiences in a media log for future use by you and your colleagues. ■

PSAS
Communication Through Public Service Announcements

Public service announcements (PSAs) are a great way to work with local newspapers, and radio and television stations to communicate information about upcoming community events and service opportunities, as well as other information of benefit to the community. PSAs are noncommercial advertisements or announcements designed to educate the public about a specific issue or cause. Radio, television, and print outlets run them free of charge on behalf of the public interest. These messages must contain information beneficial to the community and cannot include controversial material.

PSAs can take a variety of forms and can be produced free of charge with a little thought and creativity. You should explore how PSA radio reader scripts, community calendar listings, and customizable print PSAs can be used year round to promote your program and activities.

PSA READER SCRIPTS

A PSA reader script is a short script that radio announcers read live on the air or record for later broadcast on a radio station. Most often, this type of PSA is used to fill open airtime with relevant announcements and messages that connect with the community.

Writing style

When writing a script, remember that broadcast copy is written and designed for the ear. Your broadcast copy should:

> Sound personal and have a sense of immediacy

> Be clear, concise, and conversational

> Contain pertinent, accurate information (correct date, phone number, names, and Web address where appropriate)

> Be written in the active voice and present tense whenever possible

> Use contractions, just as you would when talking

> Include information about how listeners or viewers can obtain more information (Web address or phone number where appropriate)

Your message should be simple and easy to understand the first time it is heard. One way to test your script for conversational tone is to read it aloud to someone else who is not already familiar with your message or event. Make sure there are no words that are hard to pronounce, and ask your "test audience" to repeat back to you the ideas or main messages they heard. Be sure to have someone carefully edit your script before it goes out the door, preferably someone unfamiliar with the subject.

Length

Stations follow tight schedules and often use reader scripts to fill unused airtime. If possible, provide stations with scripts of each of the following lengths, offering them choices to best fit their needs.

15 seconds – about 30 words
30 seconds – about 75 words
60 seconds – about 150 words

Appendix F has a sample PSA reader script.

COMMUNITY CALENDAR LISTINGS

When promoting an event, encouraging community members to attend is as important as engaging reporters to cover the story. A community calendar listing is a place where people can find out about upcoming events in their area. These calendar listings are posted free of charge, and are often printed in local newspapers or newsletters, posted on community websites, or broadcast on local radio and television stations. A listing gives a short description of the event; the location, date and time of the event; and contact information so people can obtain more details about the event.

PRINT PSAS

Print PSAs can be easily included in your print and online newsletters, and are a great way to reach out to local community papers with your message. They can be as simple as a box with your program logo, contact information and a short recruitment message, or more detailed to include a photo, body copy and other graphic elements. When designing a print PSA, there are a number of important tips to keep in mind:

> Consider your budget. Can you design something in house, or request design assistance from a program or community partner?

> Contact your community papers to find out if they will accept print PSAs, and what size and format they should be.

> Include your program logo, Web site address and phone number (if appropriate), and a short "call to action" (i.e. volunteer, come to an event, etc.). Remember, just like any other PSA, a print PSA must contain information that benefits the community.

> Refer to the Corporation for National and Community Service's Graphic Standards Guide, located at *www.nationalservice.gov*, for guidelines on logo use, colors and other graphic elements.

Occasionally, the Office of Public Affairs at the Corporation for National and Community Service provides customizable print PSAs that can be used to support your efforts. These often leave room for local program logos and local contact information. You may request these products and localize them for use in your community.

GETTING YOUR PSA PLACED

Research Media Outlets

Before pitching a PSA to local broadcast and print outlets, find out about the media organization, its programming and its audience, especially any public service efforts in which the outlet is currently involved.

Determine Appropriate Contacts

When seeking free time or space for PSAs, begin by building a relationship with the appropriate contact at each outlet with which you want to work. To determine the appropriate contact, call and ask for the name of the public service director or community affairs director. When compiling your list of contacts, be sure to collect the following information:

> Name and title

> Mailing address

> E-mail address

> Fax and phone numbers

> Specific instructions for submitting PSAs (e.g., what format the PSAs will need to be in)

Prepare Your Pitch

Pitch memos are your first line of communication with a media outlet. They introduce the outlet to your program, promote the role of volunteers in your community, and suggest how the station or newspaper can inform the community about your program or event. These memos will be the key to capturing the attention of a public service director.

Make Preliminary Calls

These initial calls give you a chance to double-check your contact information and build a rapport with public service and community affairs professionals. Always remember to keep these conversations short and to the point.

Seek PSA Placement Commitment

Often, the public service or community affairs director will not be able to commit immediately regarding the placement of your PSA. They might have to send it through a committee or wait for space to open up in their rotation. You may need to continue to call for several weeks to find out if your announcement will run.

Track Use of the PSA

Track your PSAs once they begin airing so that you know whether your community is being exposed to your messages, and whether placing PSAs is a tactic you will want to continue using. Tracking PSAs can be challenging. Media outlets often use PSAs as "filler," running them when a paid spot is unexpectedly cancelled or during time periods that have not been claimed by advertisers. Do your best to keep track of where and when your PSAs are running. ■

APPENDICES

Every year, thousands of stories about Senior Corps, AmeriCorps, and Learn and Serve America appear in the media. Almost all come from pitches made by staff or volunteers in local projects. Here are the ten most common ways that national service programs get media coverage. Try them all!

1. **Volunteer feature story** - The most common type of coverage about national service is a feature story about an individual volunteer making a difference. National service rarely generates breaking news, but every local program has powerful and moving stories about their volunteers and the people they serve. Find your most compelling story, get permission from the volunteer and service beneficiary to pitch your story, put the details in writing, and make a pitch to a columnist or feature writer in your local newspaper.

2. **Recruitment pitch** – Many news outlets are looking for ways to serve the public good, and all want to provide useful information for their readers and listeners. That's why recruitment stories or announcements are easy to place. Many newspapers have a regular column on volunteer opportunities, or a community calendar where you can announce your recruiting event. But your recruitment message doesn't have to be at the end of the newspaper. Try to get it on the front page by pitching a metro reporter about a community problem that your program is trying to solve and your need for additional volunteers.

3. **Grant announcement** – Grant announcements are an ideal time to get coverage, especially if you organize a press conference or site visit with a Member of Congress, mayor, or other elected official. While conveying the specifics of the grant, be sure to also raise it up a level and provide broader context about what your program does – and have real volunteers and beneficiaries on hand to talk about their experiences. This will encourage reporters to go beyond a short blurb about the grant and write a more in-depth profile of your project and its benefits to the community.

4. **Day of service projects** – The calendar is full of Days of Service, and every one of them is an excellent media opportunity. Whether it is Martin Luther King Jr. Day of Service, Make a Difference Day, National Volunteer Week, or something else, it's easy to get coverage, especially if you have a large and visible community project. Make sure to organize a kick-off, lunch, or closing ceremony within a specific time period so that media can come to hear the speakers, and take photos for your website.

5. **Evaluation or accomplishment report** - We know national service programs get tremendous things done in communities, but sometimes it can be hard to demonstrate the final results. That's why it's important to share any evaluations or accomplishment reports with the media. Evaluations – especially if they are done by an independent party – are an attractive media "hook" because they summarize data about a program's impact and validate what previously was known only by anecdote. Be sure to "piggyback" off of the national studies on service done by the Corporation – reporters like to have a local take on a national story.

6. **Letter to the editor or op-ed** – Letters to the editor are one of the most read sections of a newspaper, and they are easy to get placed – making them a perfect venue for your national service message. Remember to keep it short (150-200 words) and refer to an already published story. See Appendix J for more tips. Op-eds are more time consuming but also give you more column space to get your message out. Make sure your op-ed is timely, well-written, and takes a particular point of view. Tips on writing op-eds are in the appendix section.

7. **Award or anniversary** – Volunteer recognition is not just an important retention tool, it also makes an excellent media pitch. Whether it's a local volunteer recognition luncheon of Governor's service award or a national honor such as a Spirit of Service award, be sure to let the media know about your outstanding volunteers. Invite VIPs such as elected officials or media personalities to give out your awards – they'll feel good about doing it and you'll boost your chances of coverage. If you aren't already doing so, give out President's Volunteer Service Awards – volunteers love them, and it raises visibility for the media. Information is at *www.presidentialserviceawards.gov.*

8. **Seasonal tie-in** – Holidays are excellent times to reach out to the press because they typically are slow news days. Reporters are always looking for stories about service and philanthropy around Thanksgiving, Rosh Hashanah, and Christmas. Use July 4th to show how your program encourages citizenship and patriotism. Organize a visit to a veterans home or conduct oral histories around Memorial Day or Veterans Day. Beyond holidays, look at the calendar for seasonal events such as the annual "back-to-school" time to highlight your education efforts. Commemorative days and months – such as National Mentoring Month or Older Americans Month – provide another useful media hook. Look them up at *www.whitehouse.gov*

9. **Piggyback on a national story** – Many national news stories have a local angle. If the homeland security alert is elevated, you can pitch local volunteer efforts in public safety or disaster preparedness. If a big study is released on student achievement, you can demonstrate how local tutoring efforts have helped raise reading scores.

10. **Induction or graduation** – AmeriCorps inductions or graduations are very media-friendly. Invite a high profile speaker to speak, choose a symbolic or prominent location such as a state capitol, and invite the media.

If you have other tips on how you got great media coverage, please share them by sending an email to *sscott@cns.gov.*

APPENDIX B: MEDIA RESOURCES FROM THE CORPORATION

The Corporation has a variety of tools and resources to help you reach out to the media and achieve your communication goals. From websites and newsletters to training and advice, we're here to help.

Websites

All of the Corporation's websites are chock full of information and ideas to help you conduct media outreach. Go to any of our sites (www.nationalservice.gov, www.seniorcorps.gov, www.americorps.gov, and www.learnandserve.gov) to find the following:

> **Press releases:** This is your best source for the latest news about national service. Our press releases cover everything from Congressional actions and funding availability to research reports and grant announcements.

> **News from the Field:** Service happens on the local level, and now you can get news about local developments in national service in this new section of our website that has a sampling of press releases from state commissions and programs from around the nation.

> **Stories of Service:** Service can have a profound impact – not just in the community, but on those who serve. This new section of our website has profiles and first person accounts about the joys and challenges of making a difference through national service. These can be used to recruit members and volunteers, offer reporters a glimpse of the importance of service, or highlight your own programs. We encourage you to submit your own stories to us for inclusion in this section.

> **National Service News:** Launched in 1995, this biweekly e-newsletter for people in service has news, program profiles, service heroes, and inspirational quotes from the field.

> **State Profiles:** Ever wonder how many AmeriCorps members are in your state? What Senior Corps projects you have? How much total funding comes from the Corporation? State Profiles can answer these questions and more. These reports list participants, sites, and funding for all national service projects in your state – a handy tool for working with media, funders, and elected officials.

> **Research:** Visit the research section of our website for the latest evaluations and research findings about national service. Reports such as the AmeriCorps Longitudinal Study or the Senior Companion Impact Survey provide a national context for your local project and give you an opening to talk to media in your area.

> **Photo library:** Need a photo for a brochure, news event, or presentation? Visit our photo library to browse over 150 photos of national service participants in action. If you see something you like, we'll send a high-resolution copy for your publication or website. It's free and easy.

Communicators Network

In 2004, the Office of Public Affairs created an email distribution group for people in the national service network whose duties in whole or in part include communication. Members of the "National Service Communicators" email group receive press releases, weekly electronic press clippings about national service, advance notice of upcoming press opportunities, media tips and more. To join the network, please send an email to sscott@cns.gov.

Public Service Announcements: Learn about our latest PSA campaigns and access materials designed to help you implement activities to engage radio, television, and print media in your local community.

Staff

Have a question or needs some advice about working with the media? Call the Office of Public Affairs at 202-606-5000. While our staff is small, we'd be happy to answer your questions and direct you to resources that can help.

APPENDIX C: TIPS ON WRITING A PRESS RELEASE

The press release is the most widely used tool in obtaining media coverage—whether it's print, radio, or television coverage. A press release should provide the news you want released to the media and read exactly how you'd like your news to be reported. Here are five basic tips on how to write a press release:

1. **Put your reporter cap on** – The press release should be written from a reporter's perspective. Focus on the facts and provide as much information on what reporters (and their audience) want to know: who, what, where, when, why, and how.

2. **Use the "inverted pyramid"** – Be sure to organize your information in the "inverted pyramid" style of writing. Arrange your release so that the most important facts appear first, followed by supporting facts in the order of importance to your story. This is especially important because reporters always cut from the bottom up.

3. **Come up with a good headline** – The headline of your press release is what will either grab a reporter's attention, causing them to read more, or give them reason to toss the release aside. Be sure to make it compelling so the reporter or editor takes notice.

4. **Focus on the lead paragraph** – The lead paragraph is the most important element of your release. It summarizes the news you are releasing and is meant to reel in the reporter. The lead should be kept short—no more than one to two sentences. Be sure you don't bury your lead in the body of the press release. Other important elements of a press release include:

   > **Quotations** – Quotations from spokespeople bring your story to life and give your release a voice. Quotes allow you to state an opinion and editorialize your news. Always be sure to obtain sign-off from the person you are quoting.

   > **Notations** – It is customary to include the word "more" at the bottom of the first page of a release if it's longer than one page. At the end of the press release, be sure to include one of the common end notations (### or -30-). This way, an editor knows that there is no more information.

   > **Boilerplate** – Don't forget to include standard language to describe your organization at the bottom of every press release after the end notation. If you reference the Corporation for National and Community Service, be sure to use our boilerplate: The Corporation for National and Community Service provides opportunities for Americans of all ages and backgrounds to serve their communities and country through three programs: Senior Corps, AmeriCorps, and Learn and Serve America. Together with the USA Freedom Corps, the Corporation is working to build a culture of citizenship, service, and responsibility in America. For more information visit www.nationalservice.gov.

5. **Proofread** – Always proofread a press release; do not rely on spell-check alone. It is helpful to have another person look over your press release before distributing it to media outlets.

APPENDIX D: TIPS ON HOW TO STAGE A SUCCESSFUL MEDIA EVENT

A media event involves inviting the media to a news conference or an activity (i.e., service event or fundraiser).

What should you think about when planning a media event?

> **What:** You should decide upon an event based on the message you want to get across to the media and the community, and your organization's resources. Hold a news conference if you have an announcement to make. If you want to get more people involved in your organization, plan a service event. However, you can certainly combine two types of events if you wish to accomplish a variety of things.

> **When:** Choose a date that works for the types of people you want to draw. For example, if you want families to participate, choose a weekend day. However, it is easier to get media involvement during the week, as newspaper, radio, and TV outlets only retain skeleton crews over the weekend. Keep in mind that the best time to schedule a media event is midday, ideally between 10:00 a.m. and 1:00 p.m.

> **Where:** Make sure to pick a location that is well-known and easily accessible. Holding your event in a central location, near the media, will help facilitate coverage. If you are holding a stand-up news conference in conjunction with a service activity, make sure the service activity serves as the backdrop to the event. Ideally, the location will add relevance. For example, hold the event near a city or town hall if you want to get the attention of elected officials. If you are thinking about holding your event outdoors, consider the weather. For example, a blazing summer sun may not be ideal for a news conference or a service event.

> **Who:** Your organization's activities should be the focus of the event. You can also work with other groups and agencies to demonstrate a community-wide effort. The media always takes an interest in the human side of an issue, so look for a person or family that has a positive story to tell about their community service experience with your organization. Consider inviting community leaders, such as the mayor, City Council members, faith leaders, or business leaders, to speak at a news conference.

What should the event look like?

> **Signage:** If you include a Corporation for National and Community Service logo with your local banner, it will reinforce the message that your organization is part of a nationwide service agency. Hang posters and banners in the most visible place possible. Cameras will want to get footage of the news conference or service event, and the banner should be in that shot. Display the banner: 1) behind speakers at a news conference; 2) behind or around a service event; or 3) in the entrance of the building where the news conference or other event is being held.

> Template podium sign designs with both your organization's logo and the Corporation's logo should be placed within camera view on the speakers' podium.

> **Action and visuals:** Recruit people to get the word out and attend your event. You need a lot of people and activity to show that the event is a success. You'll want to show the media not only the important people at an event, but all of your organization's volunteers and service participants.

Who should communicate your program's core messages?

> **Spokespeople:** Assign one or two spokespeople to communicate the message at the event. Make sure that they have been briefed beforehand. They should be on hand to respond to the media, convey the messages, and describe your organization and the programs that you put forth. Consider recruiting the participation of a spokesperson who speaks other languages that are frequently spoken in your community. It is also important to include participants who have had positive experiences working with your organization.

Commemorating [X] Years of Service to the [X] Community

IN OUR COMMUNITY

• [PROGRAM] has provided [LIST SERVICES].

• [PROGRAM] volunteers have contributed [X] hours over [X] years.

• More than [X] people have been helped by [PROGRAM] over the past [X] years.

• Over the past [X] years, more than [X] people have volunteered their time and energy in the [CITY] community.

• Since [PROGRAM'S] inception in [YEAR], it has expanded to serve more than [X] people.

• In the next [X] years, [PROGRAM] plans to serve more than [X] people and continue to offer [SERVICES] in the community.

IN OUR STATE

[GET STATE SPECIFIC INFORMATION FROM THE STATE PROFILES AT *WWW.NATIONALSERVICE.GOV*]

ACROSS THE NATION

> **Senior Corps**

• More than 500,000 individuals volunteer through Senior Corps each year.

• More than 100 million volunteer service hours are contributed annually through Senior Corps.

> **AmeriCorps**

• More than 400,000 have served through AmeriCorps.

• More than 2,550 charities and nonprofits have participated in the program.

• More than $1 billion in AmeriCorps Education Awards have been earned by individuals serving in AmeriCorps.

> **Learn and Serve America**

• Learn and Serve America is the largest national funder and resource for service-learning programs. It supports thousands of teachers and programs that engage young people in service to their community as part of their education and development. This year, an estimated 1.8 million students participated in projects supported by Learn and Serve America.

[PROGRAM]   Start Using: Upon Receipt
[ADDRESS]   Stop Using: [DATE]
[CITY], [STATE] [ZIP CODE]

CONTACT: [NAME]
XXX-XXX-XXXX

(30 seconds)

[PROGRAM] is making a difference in our community.

In [CITY], [PROGRAM] is increasing the literacy rate
by tutoring children and teaching adults how to read.

If you're [PROGRAM AGE REQUIREMENT], you can become
a [PROGRAM MEMBER] and make a difference in your community.

Help someone in need.

[Apply your –OR– Get] life experience.

Log on to *www.nationalservice.gov* or call XXX-XXXX
for more information.

MEDIA ADVISORY

[DATE]   CONTACT: Name
                                                    [PHONE]
                                          [E-MAIL ADDRESS]

[LOCAL PROGRAM] Holds [TYPE OF EVENT] to Highlight [YOUR MESSAGE]

[HIGHEST RANKING OFFICIAL/PARTICIPANT] will [DO WHAT AT EVENT] with community members

OR

Local community members join forces with [LOCAL PROGRAM] to [ACCOMPLISH WHAT IN THE CITY]

This [DATE], more than [NUMBER OF VOLUNTEERS/MEMBERS/ PARTICIPANTS] from [PROGRAM NAME], a grantee of the Corporation for National and Community Service, will [DESCRIBE SERVICE EVENT].

Since 1994, the Corporation's Senior Corps, AmeriCorps, and Learn and Serve America programs have engaged millions of Americans of every age and walk of life in volunteer service to meet vital needs in communities throughout the country. [LOCAL PROGRAM] has provided [LIST SERVICES] and engaged more than [X] volunteers in service to the community.

In [STATE/COUNTY/CITY], [LOCAL PROGRAM] will [EXPLAIN YOUR REASON FOR HAVING EVENT – GAIN MORE VOLUNTEERS, MARK A SUCCESS, CELEBRATE SERVICE, ETC.]. Members of the community are invited to attend and participate.

> What: [EVENT/SERVICE ACTIVITY] to:

  • [DESCRIBE SERVICE EVENT]

  • Provide information about [LOCAL PROGRAM] to interested individuals

  • Link [LOCAL PROGRAM] to the Corporation for National and Community Service

> Who: [HIGHEST RANKING SPEAKER/PARTICIPANT]

  • [PROGRAM DIRECTOR]

  • [NUMBER OF VOLUNTEERS] volunteers from [LOCAL PROGRAM]

> Where: [ADDRESS AND DIRECTIONS]

> When: [DATE AND TIME]

[DATE]

CONTACT: Name
[PHONE]
[E-MAIL ADDRESS]

[LOCAL PROGRAM] Celebrates Community Service with [TYPE OF EVENT]
and Highlights Involvement with the Corporation for National and Community Service

[HIGHEST RANKING SPEAKER/PARTICIPANT] participates in [ENTER EVENT] with
community members

OR

Local community members join forces with [LOCAL PROGRAM] to [ACCOMPLISH WHAT IN
THE CITY]

[CITY, STATE]–To [DESCRIBE REASON FOR HOLDING EVENT], more than [NUMBER OF
VOLUNTEERS] volunteers from [PROGRAM NAME], a program funded by the Corporation for
National and Community Service, have come together today to [DESCRIBE SERVICE
EVENT/ACTIVITY].

[HIGHEST RANKING SPEAKER/PARTICIPANT] joined the [EVENT/SERVICE ACTIVITY]
on [DATE] to [DESCRIBE INVOLVEMENT]. Other participants included [NAME ADDITIONAL
PARTICIPANTS].

"For [ENTER YEARS IN EXISTENCE] years, [PROGRAM NAME] has helped [LOCAL
COMMUNITY] to [DESCRIBE APPROPRIATE ACTIVITIES AND HIGHLIGHT
ACCOMPLISHMENTS]," said [HIGHEST RANKING SPEAKER/PARTICIPANT]. "Thanks are
due to the Corporation for National and Community Service, which funds [LOCAL PROGRAM]."

Across the country, the Corporation for National and Community Service's participants in Senior
Corps, AmeriCorps, and Learn and Serve America have done tremendous good for our nation.
They have improved the lives of millions of our most vulnerable citizens by helping children learn
to read, caring for the frail elderly, rebuilding communities struck by disasters, transforming failing
schools, and revitalizing communities. They have done this both through direct service and by
mobilizing millions of additional volunteers.

"[LOCAL PROGRAM] volunteers serve our community with tremendous dedication and
enthusiasm," said [PROGRAM DIRECTOR]. "Without their assistance, we would not be able
to provide the services vital to the health and well-being of our community."

[LOCAL PROGRAM BOILERPLATE]
The Corporation for National and Community Service provides opportunities for Americans of all
ages and backgrounds to serve their communities and country through three programs: Senior Corps,
AmeriCorps, and Learn and Serve America. Together with the USA Freedom Corps, the Corporation
is working to build a culture of citizenship, service, and responsibility in America. For more
information, visit *www.nationalservice.gov.*

An opinion editorial (op-ed) is an opinion expressed in writing to be published by a newspaper. A person of authority on the subject or a person with a vested interest typically signs the op-ed. It is an excellent method to express an opinion to a large number of people and emphasize the importance of an issue in a timely fashion. When submitting an op-ed, select the appropriate signatory, such as your executive director or a prominent member of the community, and submit it to the editorial page editor of your local newspaper.

Below is a sample op-ed. Consider incorporating information about your local program or community in the section indicated below.

TRADITION OF SERVICE

President Harry Truman once said that the highest office in the land is that of citizen. Indeed, there is no role more vital and no ingredient more essential to the health of our democracy than citizenship. The United States was built by citizens who participated in, cared about and dedicated their lives to building a strong and solid foundation for this country. It is service to our neighbors, our communities and our nation that has made this country strong and compassionate. We have a rich tradition of service and volunteering and have long fostered a culture of citizenship and service in people of all ages.

And so it is with the goal of continuing the tradition of service in this country that the Corporation for National and Community Service celebrates its network of service programs nationwide. Local organizations are comprised of participants from Senior Corps, a program that provides older adults with the opportunity to serve, Learn and Serve America, a service-learning program for high school students, and AmeriCorps, which was created to provide opportunities for a lifetime of service.

Since the Corporation was started 10 years ago, volunteers in Senior Corps, AmeriCorps, and Learn and Serve America have made a tremendous impact in communities across this nation. Through service, their own lives have been changed as they improve the lives of countless others—helping children learn to read, caring for the frail elderly, rebuilding communities struck by disasters, transforming failing schools and revitalizing communities. The Corporation, together with its tens of thousands of local, state and national partners, has strengthened America's nonprofit sector, created a national infrastructure for community service and volunteering, and fostered a culture of citizenship and service.

[INSERT LOCAL PROGRAM INFORMATION, DESCRIBE SERVICE ACTIVITIES AND HIGHLIGHT IMPACT ON COMMUNITY]

However, we find ourselves at a critical juncture. Civic participation is decreasing. Participation in clubs and civic organizations has been cut by more than half over the last 25 years. Involvement in community life is down by 35 percent over the last 25 years. Now, more than ever, it is critical to support the work of the Corporation and its programs, which have created meaningful ways for millions of Americans of all ages and backgrounds to serve their communities and country. These millions of Americans serve as inspiration to others and actively recruit others to give back to their communities.

We need a renewed commitment to the ideals and actions that make our country great. Inaction is not an option. We must seize the moment, motivate ourselves, and encourage others to become active in our communities, our government and our society. We must explore a vision for the future where national service and civic participation are the common expectations and experiences of every American.

Robert F. Kennedy once said, "Few will have the greatness to bend history; but each of us can work to change a small portion of the events, and in the total of all these acts will be written the history of this generation." Our work must begin now, with each and every individual making a commitment to a lifetime of service.

###

Writing a letter to the editor of your local newspaper is an excellent way to leverage a current news event in your community. The letter allows you to generate a second day of news coverage for the event or activity and/or draw attention to your local service program.

A letter to the editor is typically sent in response to an article or opinion piece that appeared in the newspaper. Referencing the already published article will increase the likelihood of your letter getting placed. The letter should be approximately 150-200 words and should be sent via e-mail or regular mail to the editor of the opinion or editorial page. You may call your local paper or access its website to determine the appropriate contact. Sometimes, the contact for submission will be published in the newspaper.

Below is a sample letter to the editor. You will note that it is very important to customize the letter and include details about your local program.

Dear Editor:

I would like to commend [LOCAL PROGRAM] for holding [DESCRIBE RECENT EVENT AND ANY SIGNIFICANT ACCOMPLISHMENTS]. [REFERENCE ARTICLE ON LOCAL EVENT REPORTED IN LOCAL NEWSPAPER]. It is events like these that keep our community strong and encourage others to help their neighbors in need.

For hundreds of years, volunteers across the country in programs like [LOCAL PROGRAM] have done tremendous good for our nation. Programs like Senior Corps, AmeriCorps, and Learn and Serve America, administered by the Corporation for National and Community Service, have improved the lives of millions of our most vulnerable citizens by helping children learn to read, caring for the frail elderly, rebuilding communities struck by disasters, transforming failing schools and revitalizing communities.

As we honor the hard work [LOCAL PROGRAM] is doing in our community, it is an opportune time to recognize all past and present volunteers, and those who will volunteer in the future. It is a time to rededicate ourselves to our mission to serve, and explore a vision for the future where national service and civic participation are the common expectations and experiences of all Americans.

Sincerely,

[PROGRAM DIRECTOR]

Name	Outlet/ Organization	Phone	E-mail

www.ingramcontent.com/pod-product-compliance
Lightning Source LLC
Chambersburg PA
CBHW080734290526
45790CB00008B/3194